God be [signature] Chris Howard

WHY NOT NOW?

Sex or No Sex -
That is the Question!

by
CHRIS HOWARD

xulon
PRESS

WHY NOT NOW?
Sex or No Sex - That is the Question!
by Chris Howard

Printed in the United States of America.

ISBN 9781498437004

www.xulonpress.com

TABLE OF CONTENTS

INTRODUCTION

"I've been trying to hold back this feeling for a
long time.
And if you feel, like I feel, let's get it on,
Let's love baby.
We're all sensitive people with so much to give
Since we got to be here, let's live,
I love you.
There's nothing wrong with me loving you,
And giving yourself to me could never be wrong if the
love is true.
Don't you know how sweet and wonderful life can be
I'm asking you baby to get it on with me."
Marvin Gaye, 1973

When this song hit the charts in 1973, I was twen-
ty-two years old and married. I remember what
emotion and desire it aroused and what I wanted to do about
them. I suppose you may think that's because at least I was
married. The question that it begs, however, is what "Let's

Get it On" and similar songs do to the minds of young people who are not married and who are too young to handle all that sex involves.

The music and lyrics are alluring, sensual and pleading, but they capture the essence of why young people engage in pre-marital sex. They want it now; they want to feel good; and what could be wrong with something that feels so good?

"Sexual Healing," also by Gaye, is a depiction of what young people believe sex will do for them. They believe sex will fill the void of a missing parent, or replace the pain that accompanies being dumped by the one they loved who they thought loved them.

In essence, however, pre-marital sex is sex without commitment to anything other than the flesh and it does more harm than it does anything.

In this, "Sex: Why Not Now?" looks from two perspectives to answer this question: "Why should I wait until I'm married to have sex?" On the one side is that of young people who engage in pre-marital sex. Surveys, interviews, and other literature convey the teen view of "why not now" to pre-marital sex. On the other hand is the moral, psychological, physiological, and spiritual reasoning for abstaining from pre-marital sex. Biblical views and clinical and social data are used to support abstinence until marriage.

Part I regards the teen perspective on pre-marital sex. It contains information on teen sexual activity, the contributing factors, and related clinical and social aspects from a statistical perspective. Concluding this section is an analysis of why pre-marital (the "now") sexual activity is not a good decision.

Part II presents God's intention for sexual relations between man and woman in marriage. Before sharing my conclusions, I have delineated some of the consequences of pre-marital sex. Finally, I recommend actions that will aid in reducing sexual activity among teens followed with a conclusion.

My purpose is to develop a Christian perspective for teaching young people why "sex now", that is, sex before marriage, does not heal. Likewise, I hope to show adults (parents in particular) how their decisions may drive young people to take unhealthy measures to fulfill adult inattention. By this, perhaps some pre-marital sexual activities can be stymied; the spread of sexually transmitted diseases can be abated, and teen pregnancies can be reduced.

PART I

THE TEEN PERSPECTIVE

TEEN SEXUAL ACTIVITY

After raising four beautiful children and experiencing the joy, pain, frustration, elation, and everything else linked to parenthood, I am moved to try to reach young people. I hope to show them that adults understand and have experienced the dilemmas they face regarding relationships and sexual behavior. I listened to them and learned how they "feel" through the laughter and smiles, the fashion and the fun. So, the information gathered from them in personal interviews helped me to see why they believe what they believe and why they do what they do. It also provided me opportunities to share with them alternative means by which they could deal with the issues from which they seek relief.

The five testimonials in Appendix A are real. They do not include every reason young people proffer sex before marriage, but the information provided is both candid and heart wrenching. The participants are ages sixteen to twenty-seven. The stipulation for getting them to cooperate was that their identity would remain anonymous. They were not only excited about participating, but also were willing and anxious to tell their stories. They wanted to help. One advantage I believe I had was that they all trusted me. That in itself was a blessing. My prayer is that with this information, I can contribute to saving at least one teenager from the regrettable experience of pre-marital sex.

It is obvious from the testimonials that most of the respondents are females. Their reasons for "why sex now'" includes filling the void of a missing father, getting attention from the most popular and handsome boy in school, wanting to feel pretty after a parent's divorce made her feel ugly and unwanted, abusive parents, and jealousy. These decisions led to having sex with several partners. The consequences, however, are analogous to what Forrest Gump said about a box of chocolates: "you never know what you're going to get." They got pregnant, had abortions and contracted sexually transmitted diseases, dropped out of school, ruined reputations, became overcome by anger, and were abused by boyfriends or unfaithful partners. These results point to why sex now is not the way to go.

The testimonials give us the girls' perspective as needing "Sexual Healing," while survey results indicate the male perspective as "Let's Get It On!" The Survey questionnaire is found in Appendix B and its results are found in Appendix C. The survey results are not intended to cover the full gamut of sexual activity among teens, but are a representative sample of those results returned. There were twenty-five surveys issued with twelve returns, there were only four complete responses and they are cited in Appendix C. The males' ages were similar to the females who participated in the testimonials. Teen attitudes toward sex are influenced by parents, peer pressure, mass media, depression, religion, the internet, and physicians. The belief among many young people is that free sex is good as long as they "love" each other. They even say, "Everybody is doing it."

As can be concluded from this statement, peer pressure is one of the greatest challenges we face in abating pre-marital sex among teens. However, there are other factors that influence teen sexual behaviors and patterns.

Factors Contributing to Teen Sexual Promiscuity
Peer Pressure

Peer pressure is an important factor that has some bearing on teenagers' decisions about having sex. Adolescents (ages thirteen to eighteen) report that they are most likely to get information about sexual health issues from their peers. Increased pressure to engage in sex during middle adolescence is prevalent. Peer group attitudes about sex influence the attitudes and behaviors of teenagers. When asked where they have learned about sex, adolescents (thirteen to fifteen years old) put friends first, and then parents, and then the media.

The Media

Every element of the media plays into the hearts and minds of young adults and society in general with regard to sexual activity. We are exposed to sex in TV shows, radio talk shows, the internet, and any other venue you can think of that caters to public entertainment, information, and communication needs. Let's start this analysis with the television.

For the past fifteen years, the American Academy of Pediatrics (AAP) has expressed its concerns about the amount of time children and adolescents spend viewing television and the content of what they view.[1] According to recent Nielsen Media Research data, the average child or adolescent watches an average of nearly three hours of television per day.[2] This figure does not include time spent watching videotapes or playing video games[3] (a 1999 study found that children spend an average of six hours thirty-two minutes per day with various media combined).[4] By the time the average person reaches age seventy, he or she will have spent the equivalent of seven to ten years watching television.[5] One recent study found that thirty-two percent of two- to seven-year-olds and sixty-five percent

17

of eight- to eighteen-year-olds have television sets in their bedrooms.[4] Time spent with various media may displace other more active and meaningful pursuits, such as reading, exercising, or playing with friends.

Some television shows are potentially beneficial for teen viewing. For example: those that promote positive social behavior (good manners, respect for others, sharing, and teamwork); however, parents need to be cognizant of the fact that children and adolescents are vulnerable to messages conveyed through television which have great influence on their behavior. Unless taught otherwise, many young children believe what they see on television is reality. It has been proven through research that primary negative effects of television on children are exhibited through violence and aggressive behavior, sexuality, academics, body and self-image, nutrition, diet, obesity, and substance use and abuse.

Jane D. Brown, a professor at University of North Carolina School of Journalism and Mass Communication in Chapel Hill, argues that mass media is becoming an increasingly important way for teens to learn about sex. Brown's research examines the increase of sexual content directed at teens in television, movies, music, and the internet. She suggests that pervasive media portrayals of sex encourage young people to engage in sexual activity. As such, the media may be especially important for young people as they develop their own sexual beliefs and behavioral patterns and as parents and schools are reluctant to discuss sexual topics.

In the United States, young people spend six to seven hours each day on average with some form of media. A national survey in 1999 found that one third of young children (two to seven years old) and two thirds of older children and adolescents (eight to eighteen years old) have a television in their own bedroom. Many of those televisions also are hooked up to cable and a videocassette recorder (VCR).

Brown continues to report astounding facts about the impact the media has on sexual activity among youth. Sexual talk and displays are increasingly frequent and explicit in the media world. One content analysis found that sexual content ranging from flirting to sexual intercourse had increased from slightly more than half of television programs in 1997-1998 to more than two-thirds of the programs in the 1999-2000 season. Depictions of intercourse (suggestive or explicit) occurred in one of every ten programs. The programs themselves also portray untraditional and non-Christian views of sexuality: gay, lesbian, bisexual, and transgender youth are rarely represented in the mainstream media. Though the numbers are increasing, two programs airing at the time of research, "Dawson's Creek" and "Will and Grace" were youth-targeted, and featured gay characters Dr. Brown's research eight years later still concluded that exposure to sexualized content on TV, or in music, movies, and magazines, accelerate sexual activity in young teenagers. (post by BreakupGirl. net, August 24, 2010 internet; www.blogs.alternet.org/ speakeasy/2010/08/24/does-racy-tv-cause-racy-teens/)

One fifth to one half of music videos, depending on the music genre, portray sexuality or eroticism.

Although teen girls' and women's magazines, such as *Seventeen* and *Glamour* have increased their coverage of sexual health issues over the past decade, the majority of advertising and editorial content in these magazines remains focused on what girls and women should do "to get and keep their man."

Smartphone adoption among American teens has increased substantially and mobile access to the internet is pervasive. One in four teens are "cell-mostly" internet users, who say they *mostly go online using their phone* and not using some other device such as a desktop or laptop computer. These are among the new findings from a nationally representative survey of eight hundred and two teens ages twelve to seventeen and their parents which shows that:

Seventy-eight percent of teens now have a cell phone, and almost half (forty-seven percent) of those own smartphones. That translates into thirty-seven percent of all teens who have smartphones, up from just twenty-three percent in 2011.

One in four teens (twenty-three percent) have a tablet computer, a level comparable to the general adult population.

Nine in ten (ninety-three percent) teens have a computer or have access to one at home. Seven in ten (seventy-one percent) teens with home computer access say the laptop or desktop they use most often is one they share with other family members. Mobile access to the internet is common

21

among American teens, and the cell phone has become an especially important access point for certain groups:

About three in four (seventy-four percent) teens ages twelve to seventeen say they access the internet on cell phones, tablets, and other mobile devices at least occasionally.

One in four teens are "cell-mostly" internet users — far more than the fifteen percent of adults who are cell-mostly. Among teen smartphone owners, half are cell-mostly.

Older girls are especially likely to be cell-mostly internet users; thrity-four percent of teen girls ages fourteen to seventeen say they mostly go online using their cell phone, compared with twenty-four percent of teen boys ages fourteen to seventeen. This is notable since boys and girls are equally likely to be smartphone owners.

Among older teen girls who are smartphone owners, fifty-five percent say they use the internet mostly from their phone.

The word* sex *is the most searched term

on the internet today.

The internet may have both positive and negative effects on sexual health. According to one national survey of young people (ten to seventeen years old) who regularly used the internet, one out of four said he or she had encountered unwanted pornography in the past year, and one out of five had been exposed to unwanted sexual solicitations or approaches. At the same time, a number of sites, such as the American Social Health Association's iwannaknow.org, promote healthy sexual behavior and provide young people with advice on communication in relationships as well as methods for protecting against sexually transmitted diseases.

Despite increasing public concern about the potential health risks of early, unprotected sexual activity, most of the mass media rarely depict the three Cs of responsible sexual behavior: Commitment, Contraceptives, and consideration of Consequences. Although more than half of the couples who engage in sexual intercourse on television are in an established relationship, one in ten are couples who have met only recently; one quarter does not maintain a relationship

23

after having sex." Only one in ten of the television programs including sexual content mention the possibility of sexually transmitted diseases due to unprotected sex. It is rare to see unintended pregnancies, and abortion is too controversial for commercial television and magazines.

Researchers with the Children's Digital Media Center at the University of California at Los Angeles agree: "an important venue where adolescents can deal with their growing sexuality is the internet." They contend that teens use the internet to help construct their sexuality and identity. Their analysis is based on monitored conversations in an online teen chat room. Their findings indicate that the virtual world offers a safe environment for teens to explore their sexuality and learn about sex. Their research explores the idea that adolescents' online interactions are both a literal and metaphoric screen for representing two major adolescent developmental issues: sexuality and identity.

The Pew Internet and American Life Project survey, conducted in the fall of 2000, concluded that at least seventeen million or seventy-three percent of all youth between twelve and seventeen years old use the internet. Although used for

24

both instrumental purposes (i.e. school work and researching educational material) and for social communication (with friends, meeting new people, and joining groups), the use of the internet for communication purposes are more popular. Some of the applications used are chat rooms, blogs, and bulletin boards – opening a window into adolescent concerns. Thus, these researchers examined the content of an online teen chat room.

Of particular interest to the researchers in this case was the culture (that which is socially constructed and shared interactively) of the online chat room environment. Here they refer to symbolic vs. material aspects of culture, including linguistic codes, interactions, and discourse patterns found within online spaces. They were highly concerned about how the symbolic devices were used to enact important adolescent concerns online, specifically social construction of sexuality and identity. It was assumed that the culture of chat is an evolving one and is being constructed and shaped by the users themselves. The study adopted a practice perspective, focusing on a particular type of media use that is woven into the fabric of everyday activity. Participants are not only interacting with media; they are also interacting with each other.

Among online youth between fifteen and seventeen years of age, seventeen percent were participating in chat rooms. This is a statistic of the Kaiser Family Foundation survey conducted in the fall of 2001. The Pew study concluded that fifty-five percent of online teens had visited a chat room. The data here came from chat rooms where teens are just "hanging out" rather than chat rooms with dedicated topics (i.e. Virginia teens, teens looking for romance, etc.). The anonymity of the chat room is a key factor; although participants have to register before using a chat provider, it is highly probable that most of them provide false details about themselves. A user has to choose a screen name or nickname that is visible when he/she is in the chat room. Users are advised not to reveal personal information when choosing an online name. Unless users divulge their identity in conversation, participants in a chat room are typically anonymous and disembodied to each other; thus participants in a chat room generally cannot place each other in the real world, neither geographically nor by name.

Construction of sexuality is one major adolescent developmental issue. Sexual maturation during adolescence is accompanied by increased sexual drive and interest. Teens spend "time talking about sex, joking, using sex slang, and exchanging sex-oriented literature." This is how they understand and control sexual feelings. This suggests that open communication with peers can serve as coping mechanisms for adolescents needing sexual expression.

The combination of online chat rooms and peer interaction with a popular medium becomes especially suitable for adolescent sexual exploration; however, youth who participate are at greater risk for unwanted sexual solicitation. Teenagers use Facebook more than any other social media site and have over four hundred friends. Twitter and Instagram have tremendously increased usage since 2012, according to Pew and Harvard's Berkman Center. Given that peers and media are such important sources of sexual information for teens, this frequency is no surprise. However, little is known about the extent of detail teens share about sex on the internet or in general. This study's goal was to try to fill in that gap.

American children live in an "all-pervasive sexualized media environment" that produces a "tremendous amount of inadvertent exposure to pornography and other adult sexual media." Teenagers are routinely exposed to values on the internet that would disturb many parents. Often, teens search the internet for information about sex they consider too embarrassing to discuss with adults. Patricia Greenfield, UCLA psychology professor and director of UCLA's Children's Digital Media Center (CDMC) says, "not only will children seeking pornography find it all over the internet," but those not looking for it are oftentimes inadvertently exposed to it when searching for information on appropriate subjects.

Childhood used to be a time of relative innocence for many children, but with today's all-pervasive sexualized media environment, that is no longer the case. Because online participants use ubiquitous a/s/l (age/sex/location) chat codes for fundamental identity-related information about potential conversation partners, it is difficult for children to avoid highly sexualized material that is intended for an adult audience.

The natural increase in sexual drive in adolescents prompts them to initiate and engage in romantic relationships. The importance of these relationships is evidenced by finding more than one half of all calls to a national telephone hotline dealt with relationship issues. The unfortunate part is most of these new relationships are frequently accompanied by risky physical behaviors, such as engaging in unprotected sex. Physical dangers may be reduced when teens date and build romantic relationships online. This is called cyber-sex, or sexual arousal or masturbatory activity in response to interaction with an online partner. Internet dating also allows teenagers to maintain their anonymity and could lessen the emotional pain that is often associated with face-to-face dating; it may also allow girls to assume more authority in their interactions since obtaining and maintaining relationships is based on verbal skill (a female strong point).

The quest for self-understanding, or the construction of a psychosocial identity, is another major developmental issue during adolescence. This quest to find his or her unique and consistent self-definition is caused by the changes that naturally occur during adolescence. Psychoanalysis expert Erik

Erikson explains that the psychosocial task facing adolescents is to develop relatively stable and consistent identities (sexual, moral, political, and religious). Researchers have learned adolescents use the multimedia environments to express who they are and to learn about sexual and romantic scripts in their search to learn about sex and gender—two important aspects of identity development.

The body is an important means for expressing gender, sexual and other identities. However, because participants online are disembodied from each other and do not have information about age, gender, race, or physical appearance, special problems are posed using this medium.

So, how do teens experiment with their identities online? Peers and partners of adolescents play an important role in the development of sexuality and identity. The adolescent's need for close friends and desire for emotional fulfillment from friends is paramount. They form small groups of friends— usually the same sex—and enjoy talking at school and at home on the phone, by instant messaging, or in chat rooms. The clinical and social aspects of unhealthy sexual decisions among youth point to the need for adult intervention in innovative ways so young people can form sexually

healthy habits.

The Statistics on the Social and Clinical Aspects of
Teenage Premarital Sex

The 2002 National Survey of Family Growth reported

that thirty-nine percent of girls and thirty-six percent of boys

between the ages of fifteen and seventeen engaged in sexual

intercourse. These percentages increased to forty-five per-

cent for both boys and girls between the ages of fifteen and

nineteen. In 2002, fifty-eight percent of teenage girls reported

having sex by age eighteen and seventy percent by age nine-

teen. The survey also found that the number of girls who had

sex before age fourteen doubled from four percent to eight

percent of the survey population between 1988 and 1995.

Although there was a slight drop between 1995 and 2002,

from eight percent to fewer than six percent, teen sexuality

remains a significant concern.

Three in four teens access the internet on cell phones, tablets, and other mobile devices.

About three in four (seventy-four percent) teens ages twelve to seventten are "mobile internet users" who say they access the internet on cell phones, tablets, and other mobile devices at least occasionally. By comparison, fifty-five percent of adults are mobile internet users. However, this gap is driven primarily by adults ages sixty-five and older, many of whom are not using the internet in any capacity, let alone on a mobile device. Adults under the age of fifty, on the other hand, are just as likely as teens to be mobile internet users; seventy-four percent of adults ages eighteen to forty-nine access the internet on a cell phone, tablet, or other mobile device. Similarly, the 2002 National Survey indicates that teens have sex because many believe it to be embarrassing to admit being a virgin. Today's generation calls the idea of abstinence "old-fashioned." Instead of the term "fornication", we use "pre-marital sex" in general conversations. Words and ideas pertaining to God or things of God have been gradually removed from their circles of influence, much like the removal of prayer and the Ten Commandments from public school systems. The idea of sin is replaced with appealing words and connotations. For example homosexuality and lesbianism are referred to as "gay", and husbands and wives are "partners." The media influences the move from a Bible-based language to a politically correct one.

Statistics help explain why media (television) has so much influence on teen attitudes about sex. According to the Campaign for a Commercial-Free Childhood, eighty-three percent of episodes of the top twenty shows among teen viewers in 2003 contained some sexual content, including twenty percent with sexual intercourse. It also found that girls who watched more than fourteen hours of rap music videos per week were more likely to have multiple partners and to be diagnosed with a sexually transmitted disease.

The Depression of Divorce

Divorce is one of the greatest losses teenagers feel. Children experience both the physical loss of a parent and the concurrent feelings of abandonment and lack of control when parents divorce. Some teens can handle a parent's death better than they can a divorce. They rationalize there is no choice in death. Because of adolescent self-centeredness and sense of power that is inherent in teens, they feel unduly responsible for their parents' divorce, no matter how much reassurance they get that they are not responsible. Pure emotion takes over as the feelings of loss accumulate and serious grieving is necessary.

Teenagers who have a good support system and a strong sense of connection with their parents or other adults are able to grieve losses to resolution. They allow themselves to feel their sadness, anger, and hurt, and even talk about them to friends and adults if they believe their feelings will be respected. Healthy parents are crucial to this process. We are the ones who provide the safe environment in which teens can feel and resolve their emotions. We need to be on the lookout for losses that occur in our children's lives so we can help them work through loss and resolve their hurt feelings.

Often, however, teens suppress their emotions because they are simply too afraid to let them show at home. As children in our society grow into adolescence, they experience the loss of a sense of being protected, loved, and cared for. Some parents push them away with the excuse that their kids need to become independent and world-savvy, when, in fact, parents just want their own lives. Kids require energy and patience, which many parents are often too tired to provide. Teens get stuck in depression when they feel they have no one with whom to figure out life, no one with whom to communicate their anger, sadness or even emptiness that life can bring.

"The onion stays unpeeled, an abscess at the center of their soul, waiting quietly for someone to prick it open and drain it," are the heartfelt feelings of Dr. Meg Meeker, a pediatrician, author, and lecturer on teen issues. That is when teens turn to sex to relieve the momentary isolation, but it frequently leads to more loss in an endless cycle of emotional angst. Meeker tries to help teens view themselves as whole people, three-dimensional: physical, psychological, and spiritual. She explains to them that depression may start in one dimension and spread to another.

There was a time when even the word "sex" was not spoken in mixed company, that is, mixed male and female environments. Traditionally men separated themselves from women and children and women separated themselves from men and children. Children were not included in "grown folks'" conversations. Children respected elders, obeyed parents, teachers, and even older siblings. Those were the days when going out in the neighborhood, you had clean fun with siblings, cousins, and friends and upon returning home, your parents knew where you went, what you did and who you did it with. "Somebody" in the neighborhood had already called and reported on your activity–good or bad. That was the way it was. That was when the "village raised the children."

How is it today?

What is happening today is as much an adult societal problem as it is teenagers. Today child abuse and children's rights laws pit young people against parents, where youth take advantage of what society calls their "rights" and parental control is more difficult. One of the major issues of concern regarding teens today is promiscuity or indiscriminate sexual behavior, which has almost become the norm. Flaunting sexuality, no matter the preference, is just what kids do. Male and female virgins are ostracized, bullied, and made to feel guilty for doing the right thing. Peer pressure overrides unpopularity. However, a look at the consequences may reverse the pressure in the opposite direction.

If "sexual healing" is what girls seek and boys want to just "get it on," the consequences of their ill-founded decisions depict the opposite of what they hope to achieve. Good sexual health implies the absence of diseases and the ability to comprehend and weigh the risks, results, responsibilities, and impacts of sexual actions. The negative results of teen sexuality do not present a healthy portrait. Contrary to the teen perspective, these results prove why pre-marital sex is not a responsible decision. The answer to their "why not now" is that sexual promiscuity is really *"like a box of chocolates; you really don't know what you're getting until you eat one."* Here, "eat one" is intended to mean engage in sexual activity. These consequences of teenage sexual promiscuity, as reported in Adolescent Health, tell us "why not now?" Every hour of every day, two American young people contract HIV, ninety-six adolescent females become pregnant, and nearly three hundred and fifty more teens contract a sexually transmitted disease. **That is "why not now"**.

Although national overall rates of teenage pregnancy have declined, nearly one million teenagers become pregnant every year. Although women, regardless of age, income,

race, ethnicity, experience unintended pregnancy, a dispro-
portionate number of them are low-income African American
and Latina teenagers. **That's "why not now"**.

One-quarter of all new HIV infections in the United
States are estimated to occur in young people under the age
of twenty-one. Sixty-four percent of adolescents ages thirteen
to nineteen reported with HIV are females, and eighty-four
percent are ethnic minority youth. **That's "why not now"**.

As these statistics show, the consequences of not talking
about sex can be severe. Young people need to know and
they have the right to know about their bodies. They should
be educated and informed about sexual health. Yet, too many
social, political, and community obstacles keep them from
receiving the right information.

Making good choices and responsible decisions about
sexual activity during the teenage years can have immediate
and lasting implications for one's overall health. How teens
make decisions about relationships, abstinence or indulgence
in sexual activities, and protection from sexual diseases and
pregnancy are influenced by many factors. Parents, peers,

the media, and access to education and services impact these decisions and the subsequent results.

The good news is there are youth who engage in sexual activity that have friends who abstain from sexual activity. They tend to have strong personal beliefs in abstinence and the perception of negative parental reactions. Overriding all the alarming statistics is the godly perspective. God is our maker; thus, our opinions, creeds and conduct should be enlightened and evaluated by His Word. It has been reported that adolescents who are more religious hold more conservative views regarding sex. The National Campaign to Prevent Teen Pregnancy (NCPTP), a nonprofit advocacy group, argues religion helps teens develop moral values and teaches them abstinence. Sex is a challenging issue for adults, as well as youth, but the results of not talking with them about it are more dangerous. It is imperative, then, that biblical perspective is addressed.

Pediatrics Vol. 107 No. 2 February 1, 2001 pp. 423 -426 (internet) (doi: 10.1542/peds.107.2.423
Influence on Responsible Sexual Decisions, " Adolescent Health, Volume 2, Number 2,

Jane D. Brown, "Mass Media Influences on Sexuality," *Journal of Sex Research*, vol. 39, February 2002: 42-45, Society for the Scientific Study of Sexuality, Inc., 2002.

Brown, "Mass Media Influences on Sexuality.

Kaveri Subrahmanyam, Patricia M. Greenfield, and Brendesha Tynes, "Constructing Sexuality and Identify in an

2013 Pew Rersearch Interned Project by HYPERLINK "http://www.pew-internet.org/author/mmadden/" \o "Get posts by Mary Madden" Mary Madden, HYPERLINK "http://www.pewinternet.org/author/alenhart/" \o "Get posts by Amanda Lenhart" Amanda Lenhart, HYPERLINK "http://www.pewinternet.org/author/mduggan/" \o "Get posts by Maeve Duggan" Maeve Duggan, HYPERLINK "http://www.pewinternet.org/author/scortesi/" \o "Get posts by Sandra Cortesi" Sandra Cortesi and HYPERLINK "http://www.pewinternet.org/author/ugasser/" \o "Get posts by Urs Gasser" Urs Gasser, March 13, 2013

Online Teen Chat Room," *Journal of Applied Developmental Psychology,* vol. 25, Nov/Dec 2004: 651-66.

Stuart Wolpert, "Teenagers Find Information About Sex on the Internet When They Look for It – And When They

Don't, UCLA's Children's Digital Media Center Reports," *UCLA News, March 14, 2005, HYPERLINK "http://news-room.ucla.edu"* http://newsroom.ucla.edu.

Wolpert: "Teenagers Find Information About Sex on the Internet..".

U.S. Department Health and Human Services, 2002 National Survey of Family Growth, Centers for Disease Control and Prevention, *Teenagers in the U.S.: Sexual Activity,* "Vital and Health Statistics", 23, No..24, Dec 2004, table 3.

Centers for Disease Control, "Teenagers in the U.S., table 3. (Movie, Forrest Gump, 1994, Paramount Pictures,.

Teenage Sexuality: Opposing Viewpoints, "Religion Influences Teen Sexual Attitudes," (Detroit: Thomson Gale Publishing, 2006: 50-56.

PART II

SEX: WHY NOT NOW?
THE BIBLICAL PERSPECTIVE

THE BIBLICAL PERSPECTIVE

*For this is the will of God, even your sanctification
that ye should abstain from fornication: For God hath
not called us unto uncleanness, but unto holiness.*
I Thessalonians 4:3, 7

I f only teens would understand that sex is a **product** versus a **commitment**. A product is temporary; it will not last. Sex only cheapens and reduces people's value when abused. Marriage, a lifetime commitment and covenant with God, is the embracing of a one woman-one man heart.

The Scriptures reflect a cautious attitude toward discussion of the sex organs and related topics which was prevalent in ancient times. The poetic and imaginative nature of the Hebrew language and the Hebrew view of man resulted in the use of euphemisms which tended to conceal linguistically such things as the male and female organs, sexual intercourse, and reproduction. However, the subject of sex and related topics retreated with frankness in the Bible, even though circumlocutions frequently were used to avoid direct reference to the sex organs or to sexual activities. For an informed study we must begin with the beginning and search out God's intent for male and female intercourse.

How do Christians account for complaining with the world's values on the subject of sex? Do they follow God's commandments to walk in the narrow way, doing what is right, or do they walk in the broad way and do what everybody else is doing? Or, do they just do what they want to do and "forget" about everybody else? Perhaps going back to the beginning will shed light on the subject and guide us toward the godly perspective.

In the Beginning

The word sex does not appear in the Bible. However, the Bible contains numerous references to sex related topics and issues with a mixture of frankness and caution. The Old Testament contains the major portion of the Biblical teachings concerning sex. Reference is made to distinction between sexes in the creation account in the Book of Genesis and the Pentateuch contains numerous commandments related to sex and sexual acts. Portions of the wisdom literature deal with sex in relation to such diverse themes as married love (Son of Solomon) and the dangers of promiscuity (Proverbs). The Bible states that Old Testament teachings were included in the scriptures not only for the purpose of conveying redemptive truth, but also for the "instruction of believers through the centuries" (I Cor. 10:11).

The Book of Genesis depicts God's creation of the world and of man and woman. God, who is Wisdom and Almighty, created man in His own image. Think about it. Man was created in perfection from the beginning. His perfection was in his innocence. They did not know good from evil and as long as they walked with God, they did not know evil existed. God created woman because He saw it was not good for man to be alone; man needed help. The woman was created to be a helper to man and man to be a caregiver for and protector of the woman. God "brought the woman to the man" then told them to be fruitful and to multiply. He began with adults, created to procreate and to raise children in the nurture and admonition of The Lord. Thus, children were not created to multiply themselves until marriage. The idea of marriage is depicted in Genesis 2:21-25. From this, one can see the closeness of the male-female bond God intends. The verses portray the bond involves more than issues of procreation; the relationship includes companionship, intimate and otherwise.[1]

The one flesh in Genesis 2:24 stands out from its context by the way it makes explicit reference to a later time – namely when children are born and one can speak of fathers and mothers.[2] The narrator links God's original intention for creation and later practice in providing an etiology of marriage, "a man leaves his parents and clings to his wife. Similarly, we can see that God's creation values sexual intimacy as being good. Although the text does not imply that in order to be truly human, one must be married.

"One flesh" does not refer to sexual intimacy in a narrow way, but recognizes that man and woman constitute an indissoluble unit of human kind from every perspective. Hence,

---

[1] Terence Fretheim, "Genesis," *The New Interpreter's Bible Commentary,* Vol. 1, (TN: Abingdon, 1994): 352-353.
[2] The New Revised Standard Version (NRSV) is more explicit than the New International Version (NIV).

the author refers to but does not focus on the sexual relationship. Leaving one's parents certainly implies marriage in that culture, and marriage certainly entails sexual intimacy.

In this, the future stands genuinely open. All depends on what the human does with what God presents. The question of not only how, but indeed whether humanity will continue beyond this first generation remained open-ended, suspended in this creative movement. What the humans decide will determine whether there will be a next human generation. Human judgment will shape the nature of the next divine decision and the future of the world.[3] This situation is similar to our own, whereby a lack of sensitivity and concern about the ramifications of sexual promiscuity and pre-marital sex impact the world's future.

Satan's half truth (still a lie) had an evil twist (Gen. 3:7). From the time Adam and Eve yielded to Satan's temptation, their sexuality became a constant source of temptation and struggle. No longer being controlled and perfected by love has human sexuality become a strategic battleground between heaven and hell. Consequently, that which was to be enjoyed

---

[3] Fretheim, "Genesis" 356-357.

in intimacy and pleasurable faithfulness became an indicator of the extent of human rebellion. People use sexual fantasy to cope with inescapable loneliness of a tragic world racked with sin. It is the attempt to force our way back to Eden to recover what has been lost.[4] Whether the centerfold photographer or the prostitute or the partner in an affair, they all feed into the fantasy that "somewhere there is someone who will love me perfectly."

In our rebellion we refuse to accept the tragic reality that we cannot go back to Eden. So, instead of turning to God for mercy, the best we can do is to try to dull some of our pain with some form of pleasure that is within our power to control. Sexual immorality works well. It creates a false sense of life and passion that for a few brief moments allows us to escape the pain of our daily lives. Thus, we seek to indulge our twisted sexual passions to soothe the ache in our souls. In essence, we exchange the one true God for a false one. And, that is a big price to pay!

---

[4] Patrick Carnes, *Don't Call It Love: Recovery From Sexual Addiction,* (New York: Bantam Books, 1991): 57.

We are designed for desire. But God does not want us to merely deny or repress our desires. There is a close relationship between our passion and our ability to worship. Desire is what God uses to bring us to Himself (Psalm 37:4). This does not mean that if we delight in God, we will get whatever we want. It means that God is good, so loving, so powerful, so close to us, and so committed to our eventual well-being that only He can satisfy the deepest longings of our heart, but we must follow His plan. His plan is for marriage *before* sexual intimacy.

The root of the problem is not out-of-control sexual urges, but an unbridled heart that has hardened itself against the warming rays of God's grace and truth. The pleasure of illicit sex is short-lived. Satan is the one who constantly seeks whom he may devour (I Pet. 5:8), so every addition (or false god) has been designed to destroy the worshipper. Satan does not reward the desires of the heart; he destroys the desires of the human heart so there is no longer a passionate desire for anything, especially God. However, if we would only commit ourselves to living by God's design, we will become a weapon for God.

Sexual promiscuity is an effective weapon that Satan uses to rob God of glory and honor. Quite often we do not think of it that way, but how we handle our sexuality affects God and how others see Him. Whenever we participate in illicit sexual activity, we drag God into the scene with us and make Him a participant in our immorality (I Cor. 6:12-20). When we refuse to indulge in sexual immorality because of the deep joy and gratefulness we feel in our hearts for God's goodness toward us, we defeat the cause of the evil one by doing good (Rom. 12:21).

The pleasures of sexual intimacy are intended to be a celebration of marital intimacy. Within the context of an enduring, faithful marriage, mutual submission and love are the guidelines for the enjoyment of each other's body (Prov. 5:15-23; Song of Solomon 4:1-15; 7:1-8, 14). God's design for the marriage bed, however, cannot be separated from God's overall design for a one-flesh marriage relationship.

Marriage and Sexuality

Sex, as created by God, is for marriage. Marriage is a divine institution, designed to form a permanent union between man and woman that they might be helpful to one another (Gen. 2:17). Moses presents it as the deepest corporeal and spiritual unity of man and woman and monogamy as the form of marriage ordained by God (Gen. 2:24; Mt. 19:5).[5] Christianity confirms the original and sacred ordinance of marriage. The stability and purity of the Church and State have been proportionate to the popular and legal stability of the marriage relationship. The original appointment of monogamy is confirmed (Matt. 19:6; Mark 10:6-8).[6] The presence of Jesus at the wedding in Cana illustrates the teaching of Christianity respecting marriage. Marriage is more than filial duty; it is unifying. The husband and wife become one through the purity and intensity of mutual love; common interests are necessitated by common affection (Matt. 19:5, 6; Eph. 5:31). The Marriage Act is to be shared by a man and a woman who relate to each other "outside the bedroom" **in a manner that reflects Christ's relationship with His church.** The picture of the kind of relationship that God has designed to accompany the sexual act of marriage is

---

[5] Merrill F. Unger, "Marriage," in *Unger's Bible Dictionary*, (Chicago: Moody Press, 1979): 697.

[6] Unger's Bible Dictionary: 700.

delineated in Eph. 5:22-23. Most of what Paul wrote in this passage focuses on the man's responsibilities to reproduce in miniature a reenactment of the incarnation of our Lord.

God has built within a man the desire to be actively involved in the life of his wife to *draw forth her beauty.* And the woman is to actively engage all of herself for the sake of her husband. God's design is that she will experience the most joy in life by responding to her man the way the church experiences joy by receiving Christ as her bridegroom (Eph. 5:24).

The church is expected to openly trust the good intentions of Christ and to receive His involvement even when the outcome is hard to accept. Simultaneously, the wife is to respect her husband (Eph. 5:33) and hold him accountable to his calling to be the tender lover of her soul. In the process of giving her inner feminine beauty to him (I Peter 3:1-6), she will respectfully encourage him to be the man God designed him to be. God knows that it is from clean, mutually faithful hearts that the most meaningful sexual pleasure is derived.

The issues of marital unfaithfulness, homosexuality, abortion, abuse and unwanted pregnancies once seemed new in the Christian community. Today, in many ways we are repeating the mistakes of our fathers and showing our need for repentance and forgiveness of God. We are faced with a need to distinguish ourselves from those who do not know God. Moses warned the nation of Israel about falling into the sexual practice of the surrounding culture. In Leviticus 17, he expressed to his people what God had said about the dangers of adultery, incest, homosexuality and bestiality. With the detail of a lawyer, he made capital crimes of sexual contact with children, step-children, parents, step-parents, brothers, sisters, and step-brothers and sisters, and in-laws. He outlawed sexual relations with a neighbor's wife, a person of the same sex, or with an animal.

Moses made his reasons clear – all these sexual sins were common in the surrounding culture of his day. Yet, God's people were to distinguish themselves by avoiding those behaviors that had brought destruction, disease, and shame to the nation around them (Leviticus 17:3). Such behaviors, God said, would bring great harm to those who practiced them (vv 24-30). Even so, God's people did not and have not remained faithful to their God. As it was then, the people of God are still struggling to separate from the sexual behavior of a surrounding culture. God cares about sexual behavior because it is rooted in deeper issues.

In the New Testament, we are told to run from everything that gives us evil thoughts, but to cling to anything that makes us want to do the right thing (2 Timothy 2:22). God will certainly show us a way out of all temptations (I Corinthians 10:13). Sexual immorality is condemned in I Corinthians Chapter Six. Because casual sex is clearly an expression of lust and desire, it does not represent unity. Marriage is the coming together of two as one flesh. This is God's intent for marriage, thus, the marriage bed is undefiled. Engaging in sexual promiscuity is sinning against the body, the temple of the Holy Spirit.

Therefore the advantage of abstinence from pre-marital sex is honoring God by waiting for marriage. Paul, in I Cor. 7:7, alluded to the fact that everyone cannot abstain from sexual lust, or everyone is not designed to be single, because our present state is a gift from God whether single or married. He adds (7:9) that for those who cannot abstain, marriage is the answer. Marriage provides the freedom to satisfy desires, please the other, and honor God.

Sexuality expresses God's intention that we find our authentic humanness in relationship, which is why sex after marriage is significant. It is intrinsic to our relationship with God because it is a part of who we are, our identity. Sexuality involves self-image and self-esteem. More than anything else, it has to do with our capacity for relationship and connectedness in transcending our separateness.[7] It involves our ability as human beings to open our minds and hearts to one another and to give and receive emotional intimacy. Why? Sexuality is the external manifestation of the internal process of human identity.

There are those who argue, however, that there is no convincing evidence that teenage pregnancy is a public health problem. They say it is difficult to identify a biologically plausible reason for adverse outcomes of young maternal age. It makes little biological sense for young women to be able to reproduce at an age that puts their children at risk. For policy makers the labeling of teenage pregnancy as a public health problem reflects social, cultural and economic imperatives.

---

[7] William Tillman, Jr., *Understanding Christian Ethics: An Interpretive Approach*, (TN: Broadman Press, 1988): 176.

Researchers and health practitioners should think more carefully about why something is labeled a public health problem, together with the social and moral context in which it occurs and in which they practice.

British Prime Minister Tony Blair's preface to the Social Exclusion Unit's report on teenage pregnancy indicates the strength of these negative feelings:

"While the rate of teenage pregnancies has remained high here, throughout most of the rest of Western Europe, it fell rapidly. As a country, we can't afford to continue to ignore this shameful record."

"We do not agree that teenage pregnancy is shameful, nor do we believe that teenage pregnancy is (or is best conceptualized as) a public health problem."[8]

It is apparent that to satisfy sexual desire we must give it what it wants. This is the thought behind the lyrics by Marvin Gaye's "Let's Get It On," as well as those in his song "Sexual Healing." What is not always apparent, however, is that behind our physical desires are deeper spiritual appetites,

---

[8] Debbie A. Lawlor and Mary Shaw, *International Journal of Ejpedemiology,* June 2002.

which are only temporarily numbed by sexual pleasure. The real problem fueling sexual obsession is not physical, it is spiritual. At the root of our problem is a belief that we can satisfy our own hearts by taking matters in our own hands and by treating our desires and passions as mere physical appetites. Yet, in believing this lie, we are missing our opportunity for real solutions and self-control.

The root of sexual sin is idolatry. Idolatry is the worship of anything or anyone other than the One True God. The New Testament goes so far as to say that misdirected passions are idolatry (Eph. 5:5, Colossians 3:5). According to Paul, to covet (to long for that which God has not offered) is to commit idolatry. The reason is clear. When we long for that which God has warned about and we do not "hunger and thirst" for that which our Lord has encouraged us to pursue, we have honored our own desires more than God himself.

This is the danger that John had in view in his first New Testament letter with words, "Little children, keep yourselves from idols (I John 5:21)." This warning was "the final word' of a letter that appealed to its readers to love God above all else and to love one another as a sign of our love for the

Father. John realized that when God ceases to be the passion of our life, and when we do not honestly care for others with the kind of love that we ourselves have received from God, then a loss of healthy love will leave us consciously pursuing lusts that make us dangerous to ourselves and others (I John 2:15-17). These lusts are a symptom of idolatry.

This idolatry was rooted in the sin of Sodom and Gomorrah. Even though Sodom is known for its sexual sin, the scripture makes it clear that her sexual sins and obsessions were symptoms of the deeper problem of idolatry. Before falling into gender confusion and sexual abandon, the men of Sodom turned their passions away from God and inward on themselves. Ezekiel, the prophet, said that Sodom's sexual sins were the result of her errors, not the cause (Ezekiel 16:49-50, NIV). Behind her homosexuality was a pattern of choices that put herself, her own desires, and her own pleasures at the center of the universe. Sodom's men replaced God with a form of sexual obsession that could never satisfy (Romans 1:17-32). Sexual obsession occurs (inside or outside of marriage) when we become more focused on temporary physical pleasure than in finding our satisfaction in the design and desires of God. Sexual enslavement tightens its grip on us when we use the momentary intoxication of sexual pleasure to numb the restless cravings that can only be satisfied by a passion and love that God shares with those who trust Him.

God's Design for Sex

Sex, as created by God is for marriage (I repeat). The world has replaced the term "fornication" with a more "acceptable" or should I say politically correct term: *pre-marital sex*. The world wants evil to be considered as good and good to be considered as bad. Abstinence is the best form of protection from the prevention of sexually transmitted diseases (STDs). STDs are physical, social and emotional consequence of sin. God loves us and has designed everything as good for us. However, he created man as a free moral being who must choose to follow God's plan or his own fleshly desires. History is replete with evidence that man does not know what is best for long-term existence.

Christ shows us that by His own example that those who are filled with healthy love for God and others do not have to be preoccupied with physical sexual pleasure in order to be real men and women. Even without sexual relationships, Christ was the perfect example of masculinity. He was the source of strength and protection for the men and women in His life. He went to battle with the enemy on our behalf. He sacrificed His life for His bride, the church. He absorbed the punishment and insults of His enemies. He had close personal friendships with both men and women. He resisted the seduction of Satan. He was strong enough to be gently, zealous enough to clean out the house of prayer and secure enough in Himself to weep for those He loved. Although Jesus was God, He was human in every sense. Yet, He lived through adolescence and His 20s as a single who did not "need' a physical, sexual relationship. He lived as a faithful bridegroom waiting for His bride.

Although marriage is certainly not perfect and is populated by imperfect people, it is the only relationship God designed for sex. And, because of this, a man leaves father and mother and is firmly bonded to his wife, becoming one flesh – no longer two bodies, but one. Because God created this organic union of the two sexes, no one should desecrate his art by cutting them apart (Matthew 19:5, 6 NIV). God's design for marriage is not so much a command but a protection. Marriage is the best chance we have, humanly speaking, of experiencing what God intended for us in a sexual relationship.

Psychologist and author Dan Allender describes sex as "a physical reflection of what takes place on the level of the human soul. It intimately unites two bodies as a reflection of the union of two human souls. This level of union and vulnerability can be entrusted only to people who are committed to each other for the duration of life."[9] A life-long, committed relationship is the place where we can grow to be fully ourselves with another person who is likewise growing to be himself. It is the place God intended for us to risk being naked, being different, and being human. God's design invites us to sexual pleasure and sexual connectedness in a mutual relationship of care and commitment – a relationship that gives us the opportunity to become who we are meant to be.

Sex was meant to be a pleasurable and pro-creational experience, a surrender of our nakedness, differences, and shame to another person in a lifelong, committed and growing

---

[9] Dan Allender, *Intimate Allies: Rediscovering God's Design for Marriage and Becoming Soul Mates for Life* (Wheaton, IL: Tyndale, 1995): 308.

relationship. It may not always turn out that way; nevertheless it is what God intends. Peter Heitt captured God's intent in a masterful sermon wherein he described marriage:

"The marriage covenant and the sacrament of that covenant take two different, incomplete, sinful people, and bind them together in nakedness, despite the shame, as a picture of Christ and His church... What sheer and absolute insanity to vow yourself unconditionally to another fallen, sinful, needy person! You'd have to be crazy to get married! Yet, Jesus is married... Is He crazy? That's the point. He is crazy in love with you, and He is bound and determined to show you. He's bound Himself to us fallen people in an eternal covenant, knowing full well what He's doing. He's crazy in love with you, Bone of His bone's and flesh of His flesh." [10]

No other reality reveals our failures and our foibles, our goodness and our brokenness, our passion and our self-interest like sex. This is not just exclusive to teenagers but to mothers of teenagers. Our bodies are, at times, out of control. We enter into relationships foolishly, and we get out of relationships

[10] Peter Hiett, "God's Sneaky Way to Get a Person Crucified" (sermon, Lookout Mountain Community Church, Golden, CO: October 31, 2004).

foolishly as well. We hurt people and we ourselves get hurt. We are naked when we should not be, and we hide when we should not. We desperately long for someone to heal us from our sexual brokenness. And that is where we get into trouble.

When we view sex through God's eyes we see what we were made for and how far we fall short of that in human experiences. Sex, our longing for intimacy, and our hurts and hopes along the way, can lead us to the One who invites us to be one with Him. "His purpose was to create in Himself one... out of two, thus making peace, and in this one body reconcile us to God through the cross" (Eph. 2:15, 16). As Heitt states, "God is not bound by the covenant of the law but by His own covenant of grace. That is, He is bound by His own eternal nature, nothing exterior to Himself. It is unrelenting love; it is His nature to choose to save at any cost."[11]

Different Views

As in any area of life, there are differences of opinions about advantages and disadvantages of teen-agers having sex. From the standpoint of conservatives versus liberals, when

[11] Heitt: "God's Sneaky Way."

asked, "Should society be concerned about teen sex?" The contrast is obvious.

Conservatives believe sexual activity has negative physical and psychological consequences for young people and that abstinence is the only sure way to prevent the unintended pregnancies and STDs associated with teen sex. They support the teaching of abstinence until marriage and disapprove of comprehensive sex education that teaches the use of condoms to young people. Many conservatives support studies showing that students who participate in abstinence-only programs wait longer to have sex than students who do not; therefore, they are shielded from many of the dangers associated with sex.

Liberals claim that most people do not wait until marriage to have sex, so people (who are quite likely to engage in sexual activity of some kind) should learn to protect themselves from unwanted pregnancies and diseases. These liberals believe that sex education results in teens being less likely to be sexually active and more likely to use condoms. The liberals use the point that Europe and United States teens' sexual activity rates are comparable; however, Northern European teens have lower rates of pregnancy and STDs because of their access to and knowledge of contraceptives.

The battle between these two groups has and will continue to be an ongoing one. The ultimate Judge is and always will be God! The Prophet, Hosea, said God promised to reject people who lack knowledge of the truth (Hosea 4:6-7). Despite the argument, a sexual revolution has been evolving in the world for some time. Some believe the revolution is over, that commitment and intimacy are on their back. Nevertheless, pre-marital sex is risky business. It risks life, liberty and happiness and healing that the Lord has called us into.

No Sexual Healing in Sexual Promiscuity

The consequence of sex outside marriage or outside the love covenant God intended leaves wounds and scars that live long in the souls of teenagers and adults. The risk of disease, pregnancy, joblessness and raising a child without its father is too high. Sex, why not now? It does not heal the hurt, but creates more pain. A teenage girl is looking for sexual healing when she thinks that if she has sex with this boy he will love her and soothe the pain from the last boy. A mother of a teenager thinks that if she can get her husband to read one more book, he will heal the pain she feels from years of disappointment. A teenage girl hardens her heart and hates boys, believing that is the only way to deal with the pain of the boy who had sex with her once and never called again. A mother of a teenager agrees that men are the enemy and vows never to risk being in a relationship again.

In her book, "Mom, sex is NO big deal!" Sharon A. Hirsh points to the Samaritan woman as an example of out of controlled fleshly desires. Her flesh craved communion with another person. Hers was a desire to rest and to be complete in another person. She discovered that to reach ecstasy with another is all in Jesus.[12] If only young (and old) people would believe this truth, it would save them from the eventual emotional, physical and spiritual pain caused by premarital sex. Sexual promiscuity robs one of true friendships and long-lasting relationships. It promotes guilt and shame and certainly does not provide the sexual healing that young girls seek. Contrary to popular beliefs, fornication is bondage, not

---

[12] Sharon A. Hersh, *Mom, sex is No big deal!*(Colorado Springs, CO: Waterbrook Press, 2002).

freedom. It steals personal worth.[13] Although we are designed for desire, God in His infinite wisdom made it clear in Genesis 2:17, when He said, *"It is not good for the man to be alone. I will make a helper suitable for him."*

Sexuality is intrinsic to our relationship with God because it is a part of who we are, our identity. It involves our ability as human beings to open our minds and hearts to one another and to give and receive emotional intimacy. Thus, sexuality is the external manifestation of the internal process of human identity. Tillman says, "An example of how we do not understand this idea can be seen in how we discuss sexuality with you in our churches. We talk about the dos and don'ts in their sexual behavior. Behavior is stressed as extremely important, but we often forget about identity and self-esteem as a probable root cause to behavior. We must help young people, as well as adults, to understand that the creation of our identity comes from our relationship to God."[14]

---

[13] Serendipity Bible, 10th Anniversary Edition, For Personal and Small Group Study, (Grand Rapids, MI: Zondervan Publishing House, 1996).
[14] Tillman: *Understanding Christian Ethics*: 175-176.

Many times individuals try to fill the void in their lives by connectedness exclusively with other persons, but the void can only be filled by God.

Healthy sexuality moves from a personal relationship with God to the human relationship. The response we have in relationship to others is a relation of who we are in relationship to God. There is no sexual healing in pre-marital sex. It continues to be an unhealthy venture in to a Pandora's Box of chocolates. As mentioned earlier, this author noted that surveys and testimonials depict the disposition of "Let's Get It On," for boys and a desire for "Sexual Healing" among the girls, as reflected in the following lyrics from the latter tune.

"Wake up, wake up, wake up.

Oh baby, now, let's get down tonight.

Ooh baby, I'm hot, just like an oven

I can't hold it much longer.

It's getting stronger and stronger.

When I get this feeling, I want sexual healing.

Sexual healing, Oh baby makes me feel so fine,

Helps me relieve my mind;

Sexual healing baby is good to me.

Sexual healing is something that's good to me."

Marvin Gaye, 1983

The need among young girls for sexual healing is some-
times based on the unavailability or absence of the father,
abusive situations, the loneliness when parents divorce, or
the loss of a boyfriend to someone else. According to Pete
Heitt, "the key to healing—sexual healing, all healing, is to
surrender the shame to the lover of my soul." [15]

Whether we are married or single, a love for God must
become far more important to us than the pursuit of sexual
pleasure.

The tendency is a failure to see the difference between
needs and misdirected desires. We all learned long time
ago that when we are thirsty we need water; when we are
hungry, we need food; when we are tired, we need rest or
sleep. It is easy, therefore, to assume that we need to satisfy
ourselves with a real or imagined sexual relationship. Our

[15] Pete Heitt's sermon:"A Temptation from Paradise" (3/27/05) inspired
the author's writing of the story about the Samaritan woman.

culture reinforces this assumption. Industry and media have made an art of sexual seduction. We are surrounded by those who make a living stirring up fanning the flames of sexual desire. We will, however, become more resistant to the allure of sexual temptation when we intentionally focus our energy on passionately loving God and sacrificially serving others.

The truth is, however, that we do not need a kind of sexual experience that robs us of opportunity for long-term friendships and relationships. We do not need a physical, sexual relationship to be fulfilled as a man or woman. Sexual conquest outside of marriage is not a sign of freedom, personal worth, or sophistication. We must understand and show teens what God thinks about sexual behaviors that are not according to His design for desire. We must teach them that our desires must be His desires for us! His desires for us are found in His Word. We can delight in His Word when we come to know Him. He comforts us (by His Holy Spirit) with these words in Jeremiah 29:11. God means what He says when He says He will *give us the desires of our hearts* (Psalm 37:4). Sexual passion is a very strong desire, but it must be and can be bridled in light of the cost.

Premature Parenthood

Teen pregnancy and premature parenthood too often short-circuit the education process, thus preventing young men and women from preparing themselves for good jobs and establishing themselves in the labor market. Teen parents as well as their children are less likely to graduate from high school. Less than four out of ten teen mothers who begin their families before 17 years old complete high school. The median income for college graduates has increased by 13 percent; while the median income for high school dropouts decreased by 30%. Half of teen mothers drop out of high school *before* they become pregnant. Teen mothers experience a number of adverse socio-economic consequences compared to similarly situated women who delay childbearing until age 20 or 20-one. An example is 50-two percent of all mothers on welfare bore their first child as a teenager. [16]

Poverty is more often than not the result of teenage pregnancy, thus diminishing the opportunity for children who have children to enjoy the successes of today's highly

---

[16] Teen Sexuality, Opposing Viewpoints, Ken R. Wells, Book Editor, Bonnie Szumski, (MI: Greenhaven Press, Thompson Gale, 2006).

competitive business workforce. Because of these associated financial, social and economic consequences, the business community has a vested interest in preventing teen pregnancy and childbearing. In this increasingly high-tech world, teens must delay parenthood in order to take advantage of the time and resources available to them for the education and training they need to succeed.

Emotional Stress and Strain

Because of the intense and confusing array of emotions teens are already experiencing, they are particularly vulnerable to the negative effects of early sexual experiences. Sexual involvement only makes the feelings more intense and confusing. Depression, like most STDs remains hidden and under-diagnosed, although its prevalence among teens has skyrocketed in the past 20-five or 30 years, paralleling the rise in STDs. According to Dr. Meeker, because so many victims cannot put a name on their feelings, and too many adults pass off depressed behavior in teens as part of "normal adolescence," the exact numbers are not known. Other teenagers are so depressed they lack the energy, desire or motivation to seek professional or any other help. Thus, while physical pain drives patients to physicians, emotional pain keeps them away.

In spite of unknown cases of teen depression, the numbers that are known are terrifying. Dr. John Graydon, professor of Psychiatry and Neurosciences at the University of Michigan, one in eight teenagers is clinically depressed and most teens' depression goes undetected. Because the rates of completed suicides among adolescents have skyrocketed 200% in the past decade, suicide now ranks as the third leading cause of teenage death, after accidents and homicides (both of which could involve depressed teens, who drink and engage in violent behavior to anesthetize their feelings of depression).

"I believe...strongly that there is a correlation between the explosion in sexual activity and the epidemics of STDs and depression in our teenagers." These are the words of Meg Meeker, a pediatrician, author and lecturer on teen issues. She believes depressed teens often turn to sex for comfort, and teens who are sexually active frequently become depressed. Parental divorce, which often pushes teens into sex at an early age, is one reason for teen depression. She further comments, "as a doctor, I can probe, culture, prescribe antibiotics, and aggressively treat and tract contagious STDs, but depression is different. It's more elusive, yet equally, if not more, dangerous. It can come and go, or it can settle in, making itself so comfortable in an adolescent's psyche that it nearly is impossible to extricate. There, just as many STDs do, depression causes permanent damage that may not become apparent for years. Too many teenagers' depression can make them feel as though another entity has moved into their body; taking over everything they think, feel and do. For the thousands of teens I've treated and counseled, one major cause of depression is sex.

Just as any doctor, therapist, or teacher who works closely with teenagers and they will tell you: Teenage sexual activity routinely leads to emotional turmoil and psychological distress. Beginning in the 1970s, when the sexual revolution unleashed previously unheard of sexual freedoms on college campuses across the country, physicians began seeing the results of this "freedom." This new permissiveness, they said, often led to empty relationships and to feelings of self-contempt and worthlessness. All, of course, are precursors to depression."[17]

Another frightening fact is teens today are more likely to succeed in killing themselves in their first attempt. A study found that completed suicides among ten to 14 year olds increased from 80% from 1976 to 1980 and 100% for age 15 to 19. From 1980 to 1997, the suicide rate increased by 11% for ages 15 to 19 year olds; 105% in African American teen boys and a startling 109% in 10 to 14 year old children.

More sobering than those statistics is for every adolescent who succeeds in committing suicide, 50 to 100% attempt it. A 1995 study found that a staggering 33%% out of every 100 high and middle school students said they thought of killing themselves! Authors of one study prompted all physicians to screen every teen with an STD for depression because of the strong link between STDs and depression, STD or not.

Results of a nationwide survey shows there are substantial differences in emotional health between teenagers who are sexually active and those who are not. A full quarter (25.3

---

[17] Meg Meeker, *Epidemic: How Teen Sex is Killing Our Kids*, Washington, DC: Lifeline Press, 2002.

percent) of teenage girls who are sexually active report they are depressed all, most, or a lot of the time. By contrast, only 7.7% of teenage girls who are not sexually active report they are depressed all, most, or a lot of the time. Thus, sexually active girls are more than three times likely to be depressed than are girls who are not sexually active.[18] Some 8.3 percent of teenage boys who are sexually active report that they are depressed all, most, or a lot of the time. By contrast, only 3.4 percent of teenage boys who are not sexually active report that they are depressed all, most, or a lot of the time. Thus, boys who are sexually active are more than twice as likely to be depressed as those who are not.

Community Repercussions

Although the concept of grandparents raising the young while parents provide basic survival needs is not a new one, recently the breaking down of family has resulted in an increase of grandparents who are becoming sole providers for their grandchildren. One prevailing reason that more

---

[18] Robert E. Rector, Kirk A. Johnson, and Lauren R. Noyes, "Sexually Active Teenagers Are More Likely to Be Depressed and to Attempt Suicide," Heritage Foundation: June 3, 2003, www.heritage.org.

grandparents today are raising their grandchildren is teenage pregnancy, or unwed childbearing by teenagers. Other reasons, most of which are contributing factors in the teen pregnancy dilemma are: abandonment of children by parent(s), parental illness (mental or physical), substance abuse, unemployment, homelessness, family violence, child abuse and neglect, poverty, death of a parent and divorce.

Some grandparents perceive taking on a parental role so late in life as a blessing; they are grateful for the opportunity to form a deeper bond with their grandchildren. Others enjoy the pleasures but resent the responsibility and inconveniences involved in raising a grandchild. The grandparents' health and vitality of grandparents are affected by the responsibilities involved in raising a grandchild. "A recent report from the U.S. census (which only partially reflects the widespread nature of this issue) made the following comparison: In the year 1970, 2,214,000 children under age 17 lived in grandparent-headed households, with the mother present in half of these households. By the year 1997, this number was reported as 5,475,000, or 7.7% of all children in the United States. The majority of children are being raised by two grandparents, or a grandmother alone, with different degrees of parent involve-ment. Since then, the number has increased substantially. The rise in grandparent-headed households reflects both a parent's understandable need for help with children and, in the worst case *parental failure.*[19]

Other Risk Factors

Most primary care physicians feel comfortable dis-cussing sex with their teen patients. According to Jeffrey K. Clark, Rebecca A. Brey, and Amy E. Banter, doctors play an important role in reducing risky sexual behavior among teens and directing them to resources that promote healthy sexual behavior. Clark and Brey are associate professors in the Department of Physiology and Health Science at Ball State University. Banter is a physician and Associate Director of the Family Practice Center at Ball Memorial Hospital in Muncie, Indiana.[20] In their research, the Centers for Disease Control and Prevention (CDC) indentified risky sexual behavior as one of the six health behaviors among youth. In

---

[19] Grandparents Raising Grandchildren – From "The Grandparent Guide" (by Dr. Kornhaber) on "Raising Grandchildren."
[20] **January 2003,** www.patientcareonline.com

2001, nearly 46% of youth in the U.S. had engaged in sexual intercourse and more than 14% had four or more lifetime sex partners. Approximately 58% used a condom and 17% used birth control during their last intercourse.

Risky sexual behavior patterns which are often established before adulthood may correlate with other risk behaviors such as drug use and delinquency, which form a "risk behavior syndrome." Evidence of risk behavior syndrome suggests that multiple risks should be addressed in addition to prevention programs.

FINDINGS

Sex Education in High Schools

Our public school systems are becoming playgrounds for the advancement of a homosexual agenda. These widespread efforts include pink triangles in classrooms, grade school studies of "gay" history, transvestite speakers, school-wide events celebrating homosexuality, and student activists spreading propaganda through school publications. Likewise, legislatures are calling for homosexual indoctrination in schools. Linda P. Harvey, president of Choice of Truth, which is a project of Mission: America, a conservative evangelical advocacy group, argues that public high schools are being used to indoctrinate students into homosexuality.

Gay-friendly teachers are distorting historical facts to promote positive views about homosexuals, is her contention.[21]

Harvey believes teachers who are openly gay could sexually molest students and are bad role models. She feels gay student support groups at high schools are used by older teens to lure younger students into having sex with them.

Similarly, a new sex education program for eighth and tenth graders in Montgomery County, MD Public Schools is being attacked by conservatives for allegedly advancing a homosexual agenda. The chairman of the advisory committee that drew up the sex education curriculum is a homosexual activist whose writings on a religious website include, "Gay Marriage, A Jewish Perspective." The revised curriculum was to be piloted in three county middle schools and three high schools in mid-April [2005] and then evaluated in June. The curriculum called for, among other things, a condom demonstration and video and information about "sexual variation." This new curriculum proposes to encourage children as early as 13 to self-identify their sexual preference in school. In

---

[21] Linda P. Harvey, "Homosexual Agenda Escalates in Public Schools," www.Newswithviews.com, July 15, 2001. Copyright © 2001 by Newswithviews.com

essence, this curriculum proffers that same-sex experimentation among adolescence is normal and should not be discouraged." Attempts by some members on the Montgomery County Board of Education's advisory committee "to balance the information with recommendations from other organizations like various mainstream churches" were denied. Instead, he said, the curriculum was "pushed through pretty much without a whole lot of exposure or discussion from parents."[22]

Some parents are taking their children out of the schools affected by these controversial programs; however, retreating into religious and conservative conclaves is not the answer. More parents need to get involved and become educated and aware of what is going on in our educational systems. Contact with schools, and joining with other concerned citizens to make the right changes would be a good beginning to the end the mess we have allowed to be created.

Sexual activity among teenage boys declined after increasing 32% between 1986 and 1991. The teen birth rate for fathers aged 15 to 19 remained fairly constant until 1994, and then decreased 16 percent between 1994 and 1999.

---

[22] Linda P. Harvey: "Homosexual Agenda Escalates in Public Schools.

However, in 2009 the best available date showed the birth rate among teens was at 52%, the highest among 28 countries. Approximately 168,000 babies born to teen mothers in 1999 had fathers under 20 years old. Eight out of ten teen fathers do not marry the mother of these children. Absent fathers of teen-aged mothers pay less than $800 annually for child support, often because they are quite poor themselves! Research suggests teen fathers have lower levels of education and suffer earning losses of ten to 15 percent annually than teens who do not father children.

Boys are getting more public attention nowadays regarding their responsibility in the prevention of teen pregnancy. In 2000, at least 40 states were reported to have strategies to prevent unwanted or premature fatherhood. Although this trend is welcome, still, too many young men are not waiting until they are ready (emotionally and financially) to become fathers. The following facts make it evident that there is so much more that needs to be done to increase the numbers of teen boys and young men who do wait until they are ready to become responsible fathers. They need to be taught the responsibilities that come with marrying their babies' mothers and provide for their families physically, emotionally, financially, and most ignored, spiritually. With all this said, spiritual readiness is the most important factor in all of this documentation.

Lack of Research on the Impact of Religion on Sexual Behavior

The National Institute of Child Health and Human Development reported in 2003 that strong religious views decrease teen sex. Teens, particularly girls, with strong religious views are less likely to have sex than are less religious teens, largely because their religious views lead them to view the consequences of having sex negatively. The likelihood of adolescents engaging in early sex is decreased by shaping their attitudes and beliefs about sexual activity. Because the state of research in the area of religiosity and teen sexual behavior is generally poor, there is little to conclude on the subject. In their examination of 50 studies, Brian Wilcox, Ph.D., Sharon Scales Rostosky, Ph.D., and their colleagues find support for the idea that variously defined religiosity is associated with delayed sexual activity among some groups of teens. They also find that some religious teens are less likely to use contraception when they begin sexual activity.[23]

The lack of strong theoretical research and longitudinal studies in this field makes it difficult to accurately measure the total effect of religiosity on sexual behavior. However, there is value in further exploring the connections between religion and teen sexual behavior, because the potential for faith and religion to reduce risky sexual behavior is promising. This report has raised as many questions as it has answered. Wilcox and his colleagues found that religious affiliation, faith, and practice appear to be related to teen sexual behavior. Unfortunately, because of the weakness of the research they had no way of determining exactly how and under what circumstances this is true.

Exciting and innovative programs exist in faith communities around the United States, but we know almost nothing about the effectiveness of these interventions. It would be beneficial to both faith communities and to the broader society to learn more about how these efforts work, especially with

---

[23] National Institute of Child Health and Human Development, "Strong Religious Views Decrease Teens' Likelihood of Having Sex," March 2003. www.nichd.nih.gov

the current interest in public funding of faith-based solutions to social problems. No leaders, religious included, make decisions based solely on research. As a matter of fact, some of the outcomes that faith communities advocate – grace, forgiveness and salvation are not amenable to empirical research.

Parental Influence

Parents, mothers in particular, have an important influence on their teens' sexual activity, according to two studies by Dr. Robert W. Blum, physician and lecturer at the University of Minnesota Office of Adolescent Health. Dr. Blum reports teens are less likely to engage in sexual intercourse, if there is a high level of parental involvement and closeness.[24]

Blum and some of his colleagues conducted a longitudinal survey on adolescent health.[25] They found that teens who reported more satisfaction in their relationship with their mother were less likely to report having sex in the subsequent year,

---

[24] Robert W. Blum, *Mother's Influence on Teen Sex: Connections That Promote Postponing Sexual Intercourse.* (Minneapolis, MN: Center for Adolescent Health and Development, 2002).

[25] Colleagues, James Jaccard and Patricia Dittus, published longitudinal research from the National Longitudinal Study of Adolescent Health (add Health) from a study on parent-teen relationships.

more likely to use birth control the last time they had sex and less likely to get pregnant. The more disapproving adolescents perceived their mother to be toward their engaging in sexual intercourse, the less likely they were to have sexual intercourse. Teens' perceptions of their mothers' attitudes toward abstinence are more predictive of sexual outcomes (e.g., intercourse, use of birth control, and pregnancy) than actual maternal attitude.

Astonishingly, nearly all parents who responded to the Add Health Study were mothers, although fathers' influence is just as important. It is also important to note that teens whose mothers were highly religious were no less likely than other teens (during the one-year study) to have sexual intercourse. Another interesting observation was about 50% of parents seemed unaware that their sons and daughters started having sex. Knowing what is going on in children's lives is most important for parents.[26]

If moral values are the core of the issue of teen pregnancy, who better to involve in crafting solutions (along with parents) than faith leaders and communities? Besides public funding, there is much that community coalitions can do to help support

---

[26] http://www.grandparenting.org/Grandparents%Raising%20 Grandchildren.htm

the work of religious leaders and to harness the strengths of local institutions of faith on issues of teen pregnancy. Given the disconnect between research on the role of religiosity on teen sexual behavior and polls that show that teens rank faith leaders low as important influences on their sexual decision-making, faith communities should be challenged to do as much as they can to help teens make better, well-informed decisions about sex.

The Use of Condoms

Heather Boonstra asserts that socially conservative Republicans in Congress are erroneously claiming that condoms are ineffective in preventing the spread of HIV and other sexually transmitted diseases. While the author grants that condoms are not infallible, they are highly ranked in the prevention of STDs is her contention. She argues that relying on abstinence-only education programs, which do not include discussions of condom use, will lead to an increase in STDs.[27]

---

[27] Heather Boonstra, "Public Health Advocates Say Campaigning to Disparage Condoms Threatens STD Prevention Efforts," *The Guttmacher Report*, vol. 6, March 2003, pp. 1-6, Copyright © by The Alan Guttmacher Institute.

Boonstra is a senior public policy associate with a liberal think tank, the Alan Guttmacher Institute.

In 1999, Rep. Tom Coburn (R-OK), a physician and staunch pro-abstinence opponent of government-funded family planning programs, led a new strategy to further Congress' moral agenda of promoting abstinence outside of marriage as official government policy – claiming that condoms do not protect against STDs. They were successful in attaching an amendment to the House version of the Breast and Cervical Cancer Treatment Act mandating the condom packages carry a cigarette-type warning that condoms offer "little or no protection" against an extremely common STD, human papillomavirus (HPV), some strains of which cause cervical cancer. This directive was removed before the bill was enacted; however, Coburn and his allies were able to secure a requirement that the Food and Drug Administration (FDA) reexamine condom labels to determine if they are medically accurate with respect to condoms' "effectiveness or lack of effectiveness" in STD prevention...

The National Institutes of Health in June 2000 convened a panel of experts, at Coburn's behest, for a two-day workshop to examine the body of evidence on the effectiveness of condoms in preventing the transmission of eight STDs: HIV, gonorrhea, Chlamydia, syphilis, cancroids, trichomonoiasis, genital herpes and HPV. The panel considered 138 peer-reviewed articles. In July 2001, the panel concluded that consistent and correct condom use prevents, in addition to pregnancy, transmission of HIV between women and men and gonorrhea transmission from women to men. The panel could not conclude definitive statements specific to the other six STDs due to the insufficiency of the published epidemiologic literature. A critical conclusion in the workshop summary report that was overlooked is that condoms are "essentially impermeable" to even the smallest of STD viruses. Two important assumptions are made in the workshop report. Number one — there is a "strong probability of condom effectiveness" against so-called discharge diseases that are transmitted by genital secretions, like semen or vaginal fluid. These would include Chlamydia, trichomoniasis and gonorrhea. Number two — there is "a strong probability of condom effectiveness" against infections that are transmitted through "skin-to-skin" contact – provided, however that the source of infection is in an area covered or protected by a condom.

The report raises a number of methodological challenges that make it difficult to study the effectiveness of condoms against specific STDs. A randomized controlled clinical trial has not been used because it would require control-group participants to be counseled not to use condoms. Because this type of counseling is unethical, this type of study is not feasible, although it would be ideal. As a result of these standards for study design, the studies reviewed by the workshop panel could not be considered optimal.[28]

HIV and STD prevention advocates the imperfect status of condoms. Likewise, FDA [Food and Drug Administration] advises consumers that when used properly, latex condoms will help reduce the risk of HIV and other STDs, although no method can guarantee 100% protection. The workshop summary acknowledges that condoms must, however, remain a key component of HIV and STD prevention efforts both in the United States and globally. The summary states, "Beyond

---

[28] Study: Abstinence Pledges Not Reducing Rates of STDs," *USA Today*, March 9, 2004.

mutual lifelong monogamy among uninfected couples, condom use is the only method for reducing the risk of HIV infection and STDs available to sexually active individuals."

Further research shows **abstinence is not reducing STD rates:**

> Teens who pledge to remain virgins until marriage have the same rates of sexually transmitted diseases as those who don't pledge abstinence, according to a study that examined the sex lives of 12,000 adolescents.

> Those who make a public pledge to abstain until marriage delay sex, have fewer partners and get married earlier, according to the data gathered from adolescents ages 12 to 17 who were questioned again six years later. But the two groups' STD rates were statistically similar.

> The problem, the study found, is that those virginity "pledgers" are much less likely to use condoms.[38]

Meg Meeker argues in this viewpoint that condoms offer little or no protection against sexually transmitted diseases, especially the human papillomavirus (HPV). She states that condoms have lulled our teens into a false sense of safety, and she notes that while condom use has increased among teens, so has the rate of STDs. She concludes that using condoms cannot be considered safe-sex practice any longer. This nation is full of condom-mania where sexual health is concerned. Meeker says at every conference she attends, she sees parents and educators wringing their hands and considering condoms as the "solution." In the United States an estimated 400 high schools make condoms available to students; and students use them.

Condom use among teens has increased from 21% among sexually active boys between 17 and 19 to nearly 67% in 1995. Data from 1997 shows about half of adolescent girls in ninth through twelfth grades said they used a condom during their last sexual intercourse, compared to just over one-third in 1991. There has been a slight drop in teen pregnancies because of condom use; but it is no victory. During the same time period, the number of STD cases has grown to epidemic proportions.

All this concludes that there is no "safe sex" outside of marriage. Condoms do not work! Meeker goes on to explain that medically, the best that condoms can do is "reduce" a person's risk for contracting disease; even if condoms are used perfectly, 100% of the time, risk still exists. Other than HIV, condoms' safety levels are null and void. A panel of 28 medical experts in a report sponsored by the National Institutes of Health, a group comprised of men and women, practicing physicians and researchers, liberals and conservatives, trained to have their fingers on the pulse of the spread of prevention of STDs in the United States, gathered for a two-day workshop in Herndon, Virginia in June 2000, for the purpose of evaluating the effectiveness of condoms. They released their finding 13 months later.

They concluded that though male latex condoms could reduce the transmission of HIV/AIDS, *there was not enough evidence to determine that they were effective in reducing the risk of most of the other sexually transmitted diseases.* Their report caused a firestorm of reaction, ultimately with the call by physicians and members of Congress for the resignation of Dr. Jeffrey Koplan, then CDC director, for misrepresenting and hiding vital medical information that showed condoms do not fully protect against STD transmission. The group members reported, "The failure of public health efforts to prevent the STD epidemic in America is related to the CDC's 'safe-sex' promotion and its attempts to withhold from the American people the truth of condom ineffectiveness." The concept that condoms are the best way to prevent STDs is just wrong. Teens need to be told the truth about condoms. Much was made in the media recently about a study concluding that distributing condoms in schools does not increase sexual activity among young people. But what's being missed is that distributing those condoms is not keeping young people safe from diseases that can change their lives forever. This does not mean condoms should play no role in the battle against HIV and STDs, they just shouldn't play the central role – especially for kids, who are more prone to put their faith in them.

The Health/Faith Divide

There is a health/faith divide regarding teen pregnancy. Barbara Dafoe Whitehead, PhD. is a member of the National Campaign's Task Force on Religion and Public Values. Dafoe posits the question, why is it that so many efforts to reduce teen pregnancy have given only token representation to the perspectives of religion and faith? It is particularly perplexing since so many teens and adults describe themselves as spiritual or religious. Moreover, the most prevalent reason teens give for not participating in sex *is their faith*.

According to Whitehead much of the gap between health and faith can be attributed to a fundamental difference between the languages of the faith and public health arenas as they regard sexuality. Even when they agree on such goals as abstinence, the two camps draw from very different traditions and values to describe why teens should adopt the behavior. There is great diversity in opinion among faith communities on issues of teen sexuality.

Helping adolescents sort out their feelings, make decisions about behavior and risk reduction, understand the consequences of their behavior, and identify resources to assist in promoting positive health behavior should be the main goal of sex education. Of course, these skills can be incorporated with other preventive health messages. Physician recommendations on individual adolescent behavior change are powerful in the health education arena. Health educators could contribute to the use of their power and influence on adolescents by encouraging their support through communication and providing opportunities for interaction with adolescents outside of the physician's office. The school sport physical program is a great opportunity for scheduling time for physicians to conduct comprehensive, personalized interaction that could create an environment for sexuality issue to be addressed. Health educators can assist physicians by providing information that communicates prevention messages to adolescents. Though the involvement of the health educators and physicians are on different levels, the goal of both is ultimately the same: to improve and maintain healthy sexuality among youth. A collaboration of these two professions can make a difference in reducing risk behavior in adolescents.

It has been discovered that it is easier to help teens appreciate the reality of teen pregnancy than the reality of the epidemic of STD in the U.S. today.[29] There are four basic reasons:

---

[29] Shepherd Smith, "The Truth Must Get to Teens About STDs," The Institute for Youth Development, March 1, 2004, www.youthdevelopment.org

1. Teens hear more about pregnancy. Parents have been on the bandwagon of curbing teen pregnancy longer than we have been trying to prevent teen STDs. We have educated them.

2. Teens cannot see infections; but they can see a swollen belly. This does not help them because they live with infections they are not aware that they have.

3. Teens are often egocentric. Pregnancy puts them out. Babies force teens to make tough decisions. They require total lifestyle change. The reality which they can grasp better than that of an STD makes them respect pregnancy more – and they fear it more than STDs.

4. Teens do not want to upset or let their parents down. Fear of telling parents they are pregnant motivates some teens to prevent pregnancy, while risking getting STDs, if they take preventive measures at all.

None of us want to deal with the shock of hearing news of the STD epidemic. However, we must face it because it is a reality. Relying on condoms for protection from pregnancy and disease has lulled society into complacency that is contributing to robbing the next generation of living a healthy, prosperous and fruitful life.

It is always painful to admit that the problem is simply a lack of self-control or a few instances of bad judgment. It is equally disturbing to admit that your problem has roots in idolatry – that you have worshipped sexual intimacy more than God, and that without a willingness to be radically changed by God, your problems will continue.

The Bible does not deal with sexual sin as a small problem and neither should we. The Scriptures tell us that there is a time to humble ourselves and run. Realizing the power of sexual temptation, the best advice we can give young people is from the Word and if that fails, to just run! Paul wrote, "Flee sexual immorality. Every sin that a man does is outside the body, but he who commits sexual immorality sins against his own body." (I Cor. 6:17).

Sexual sin cannot be corrected by promising yourself to do better next time. It can be dealt with only by honestly getting to the root of one's heart desire, coming clean with God and those you've hurt, and then redirecting your heart to God. The recommendations contained in the next section are meant to aid in getting the focus to young people.

RECOMMENDATIONS AND CONCLUSIONS

The only way to keep young people safe is to tell them the truth – about STDs and condoms. And tell them we know they are capable of, and we expect them to, avoid sexual activity. Most people do not realize it, but today a majority of high school students do not have sex and the numbers are growing. The government did a dangerous disservice to America's teens when it incorrectly called condoms "highly effective." Research shows that the only way young people can be safe from an STD epidemic is to wait. Fortunately, more and more teens are making just that choice!

Reducing teen pregnancy decreases out-of-wedlock childbearing and increases the percentage of children born to married couples. Unmarried families are first formed more frequently among teenagers, even though the majority of

non-marital births are to adult women. The following statistics reinforce the urgency to devise methods that would
reduce teen childbearing. Although only three out of ten
out-of-wedlock births in the U.S. are to teenagers, nearly
half (48%) of all non-marital *first* births occur to teens – the
largest single group. Nearly 80% of teen births are to unmarried teens, up to 15% in 1960. Men and women today marry,
on average, three to four years later than did their counter-
parts in the 1950s. As a result of later marriage and both earlier menarche and earlier age of first sex, teens today begin
having sex roughly eight years before marriage.[30]

In conclusion, helping more women reach adulthood
before bearing children would certainly increase the number
of children that would grow up in more stable, married families. The benefits of children that grow up in these families, according to this research, are definitely linked to the
reduction of teen pregnancies and improving overall child
well-being.

---

[30] Jeffry K. Clark, Rebecca A. Brey, and Amy Banter, "Physicians as
Educators in Adolescent Sexuality Education," *Journal of School
Health, vol. 73*, December 2003, pp. 389-91.

Reducing teen pregnancy also contributes significantly to the goal of promoting responsible fatherhood. Research shows that involved and committed fathers are important to the well-being of their children. But unfortunately, children born to teen parents are often denied a close connection with their father because the relationship between their parents is more likely to dissolve over time. Children who live apart from their fathers are five times more likely to be poor than children with both parents at home. Boys and girls without involved fathers are twice as likely to drop out of school, twice a likely to abuse alcohol or drugs, twice as likely to end up in jail, and nearly four times more likely to need help for emotional or behavioral problems.[31] Over two decades of research confirms that parents – both fathers and mothers – are an important influence on whether their teenagers become pregnant or cause pregnancy.

---

[31] Clark, Brey, and Banter: "Physicians as Educators in Adolescent Sexuality Education."

PARENTAL EDUCATION

We need parenting education. A 2002 National Longitudinal Survey on Adolescent Health showed that teenagers are less likely to start having sex when their mothers are involved in their lives [and] have a close relationship with them. This is a key factor if our training methods are to curtail the growing tide of pre-marital sex. Dafoe notes at least three ways faith leaders and communities play an important role in preventing teen pregnancy as follows:

- They help young people develop mentally and spiritually by transmitting the teachings and observances of their faith.

- They engage in activities that guide and protect young people and give them hope for the future – including offering education, youth groups, summer camps, youth sports leagues, tutoring programs, rites-of-passage observances, mentoring, and after school programs. These youth development activities give teenagers productive things to do, offer them opportunities to gain knowledge, skills, and confidence, and, perhaps most importantly, connect them to caring adults.

• Some faith organizations explicitly address the issue of teen sexuality within the context of faith through sex and abstinence, education, parent/child communication workshops, crisis pregnancy counseling, and referrals to family planning services.

The Challenge to the Church

Faith communities have additional strengths to offer in battling pregnancy. Supporting hard-to-reach new immigrant parents and their children, high-risk teens, particularly young males, and building community-based coalitions across faiths and between faith groups and secular youth organizations are among those strengths.

Whitehead finally offers hope that the divide between faith and public health is bridgeable. Her suggestion is that adults look to teens that do not usually draw clear distinctions between the requirements of the body and the soul, for inspiration on how to bring the insights, perspectives, and efforts of faith communities to the broad-based campaigns to reduce teen pregnancy in the U.S. While the body of Christ (the church) must follow every whim of cultural change, they must be sensitive to its culture and be prepared to respond to change, especially as that change and culture deals with pre-marital sex and its ramifications.

Community Involvement

Many organizations help adolescents develop healthy sexuality. A variety of sources, such as family, peers; school, faith-based organizations, media and medical facilities are available to adolescents. The physician's role as a sex educator is often overlooked, even though parents and teens are united in wanting physicians to take a proactive role in the education regarding sexual risk behavior.

Although there is little evidence of the effectiveness of physicians influence on adolescents' high-risk sexual behavior, consistent evidence has shown that American adults have changed their behavior in response to information about HIV and other STDs through public education and medical contact. Patient education about lifestyles has proven to be helpful not only in sex-related issues, but physician counseling relating to smoking cessation and HIV has increased the reduction of risky behaviors. It has been estimated that it takes only four to seven minutes to incorporate such a positive message. Parents and teens consider physicians and school-based clinics as credible sources of sexuality information.

Physicians would do well to develop a comfortable relationship with adolescents regardless of the practice setting. Some traditional ways physicians can establish rapport with teens are: educational and social interaction at schools, establishing and working with clinics, and speaking events. Time constraints and lack of reimbursement for services often create barriers to these approaches.

Nevertheless, physicians should explore ways to increase the comfort level of their adolescent patients in the clinical setting.

Sexual passion is very strong, but it can be bridled by a passionate obedience to Christ that is more than mere dutiful compliance to the letter of the law. A deeply felt hunger and thirst for God (Ps. 42:1-2) can help us to see one another through His eyes rather than through the self-centered demands of blind desire. Paul, the Apostle, knew the kind of love that comes from a heart focused first on God. He gave us the final tribute to love ever written in I Cor. 13:1-8.

This is desire redirected. It gives meaning and direction and satisfaction to life whether there is opportunity for marital sexuality or not. When such love exists, men and women do not use or defraud each other of what is not theirs to give or receive. Certainly, such love will always be incomplete and imperfect this side of heaven.

The Biblical teachings concerning sex manifest a high ethic, especially when contrasted with the prevailing view of sex in the same period of history. The sex roles are distinguished and a division of labor commensurate with each role is apparent. However, women gained considerable status over time and the Christian view of sex allowed for mutual respect among the relationship of the first created beings. Sexual activities during both the Christian and Old Testament eras were discussed with caution and candor, coupled with relative frankness.

This study has been insightful and pleasurable. My eyes have been opened to areas and insights that I had not heretofore considered. More importantly, my heart has been opened to the plight of our young people who take on adult practices before they are able to handle them. They are like the innocents in the Garden who eat of the tree of knowledge of good and evil and find that it is too much too soon, but too late to do over. The consequences are great.

Despite the arguments, we must find innovative ways to curtail teen sexual activity. The evidence is in and it clearly illustrates that the sexual healing young girls seek is not being manifested in their lives. Sexually transmitted diseases, unwanted pregnancies, and sexual abuse are just a few of the results that should assure teens why they should wait for sex after marriage.

Waiting to have sex protects our daughters not just from disease, pregnancy, and heartbreak; it protects them for the sake of developing a sense of self. The act of sex is a surrender of self to another person. When a developing adolescent girl has sex, she loses herself, and that can have lifelong consequences. She loses herself before she really knows who she is. She loses herself before she accumulates positive choices and experiences that tell her who she is. She is

111

at risk for thinking that she is stupid, an object, inferior, or undesirable.

We need to use the awareness of our sin as a reason to run to the arms and scarred hands of Jesus Christ. Run to His cross. Cling to the truth that when Christ died, He paid the price for every sexual sin and every kind of sin that we have ever or will ever commit; and claim the forgiveness that God offers to those who trust in Him.

As we trust in Christ for that forgiveness, we must make sure that we are doing so with a desire to replace sexual sin with righteousness (right standing with God) and love.

We must teach our young people not to treat forgiveness itself as another means of avoiding pain. They must test their love by seeing if they can willingly share in the pain of those they have hurt by their sexual choices. If their repentance is real, if they really want to live in the strength of God's forgiveness and in the cleanness of His Spirit, then they will not demand that others forgive and forget what they have done to them. This is the path of real love. It is the path that allows us to walk with One who lived not for Himself and not for the moment, but for us – and for our eternal pleasure with

Him. This is the path that shows the highest sense in which we have been designed for desire.

We must understand and explain to children why sex matters and help them develop a sexual ethic. There is something about looking at this subject honestly and thoughtfully that leaves us wanting tender, loving care. That is because sex is all about desire – and letting unfilled desire take us to God. Sexual confusion, loneliness, pain, and frustration are powerful, and they will either lead us to numb ourselves, demean ourselves, and rage at others and God, or they will lead us to surrender to Him. All readers of this material should clearly understand why sex is important. For adults, may it empower them to translate the reasons to teens and make God's presence more meaningful and real.

God is the answer to sexual healing!

Appendix A

PERSONAL TESTIMONIES

Provide your personal testimony about your
feelings, opinion or advice on pre-marital sex.
What are the advantages and disadvantages based
on your personal experience?

Testimony #1

The saying, "If children aren't shown love at home they will find it in the streets," is about me. My father wasn't there for me. I really needed that attention and affection from him. My mother could only tell me about guys and sex from a woman's point of view and because no one took the time to teach her about it, she wasn't equipped with the knowledge. She only told me not to have sex. I was very curious and because everyone was telling me not to have sex and not telling me what would happen if I did, I ended up losing my virginity at a very young age.

Without proper guidance I ended up giving my body to guys who thought I was pretty and who I thought loved me. My father never told me how pretty I was or that I was special and I should wait for my husband or someone special. All he told me was not to get pregnant because he wasn't going to take care of a baby (which would be his grandchild). So, because I used sex as a crutch to fill an empty void in my heart, I ended up contracting a sexually transmitted infection that could take my life. I'm not proud of the number of guys I've had sex with, but I know that every experience taught me something and have made me who I am today; a very strong individual who has taken the time to get to know herself and love herself and to be in love with herself. I want so much for myself and I know that with God being the head of my life I can do anything. I've given my life back to him and I've had peace of mind ever since. I don't have to worry about being pregnant or if he's going to call. I've also taken the step to wait until I'm married to have sex. I'm not just going to marry anyone; I'm going to wait for the man God has planned for me to marry.

Testimony #2

At 15 years old I had my first sexual relationship. A few partners later, I couldn't even remember his name. I didn't know what true love was, but I was having fun. I enjoyed it and continued throughout my college years, just believing they loved me. In college, it was about the cars, clothes and money they spent on me. I got a lot of attention because they were popular and good looking boys. They were into the party scene and that was exciting to me. My parents were strict on us. In my mind, it was a way to get away with what "I" wanted to do. I came to my senses when I got pregnant and had an abortion to cover up the mess. The embarrassment and shame hit me when my father was wise enough to know I had had an abortion when I dropped out of college and went back home because I was ill.

Testimony #3

When I turned 16 I thought I wanted to be more than a a teenager. I wanted to feel like a woman. The boys' attention was going to my head. I actually lost my virginity inside my high school. The boy I had sex with was a childhood friend. He and I also "experimented" with oral sex in a conspicuous hotspot in the school. It was not a good experience because we were both afraid we would get caught. I was also concerned about being pregnant afterwards because we did not use a condom. It ruined our relationship and my reputation was also ruined because I did not stop with him. When other boys heard what happened, they approached me and out of guilt I had sexual relationships with them. It has been a hard lesson to learn.

Testimony #4

I'm 17 now and I can't remember how old I was my first time – maybe 15. I thought he was the love of my life. My reason for having sex was I thought he loved me. I thought I was ugly and when he told me how pretty I am, that was all I needed to believe he loved me. My parents separated and divorced when I was too young to remember. I never had a close relationship with my father, although I tried to live with him when I was about 12 years old. Because he was abusive,

I was physically abused by him. I moved back to live with my mother three years later, and we did not get along. We both had anger issues relating to my dad; I was angry because all my friends had good relationships with their fathers and I didn't. My mother was angry because he abandoned and abused both of us. I had gotten used to having more freedom living with my dad than my mother was willing to give me, so my rebelliousness caused major drama in our house. All my relationships with boys have been physically abusive except my first. He never hit me, but he cheated on me and we broke up. I am now learning to love myself and to explore what I can do on my own. I am working, going to college and living on my own. I now know boyfriends are not as important as girls think they are. I'm pursuing bigger and better things.

Testimony #5

I waited until after my high school graduation to give up my virginity to the first boy I thought I loved. My reason for having sex with him was I was jealous of another girl who liked him, and I was trying to win him over. Big mistake! He ended up playing both of us. Now as a young adult, I know

I can only blame myself for falling into the trap. My parents were strict, but very understanding and helped me heal.

Appendix B

SURVEY QUESTIONS
(BE HONEST, PLEASE.)

1. What is your age?

2. What is your gender?

3. Are you sexually active? Yes / No

4. If not, why?

5. How old were you at the time of your first sexual encounter?

6. Were you comfortable? Why or Why not?

7. How many partners have you had?

8. Would you advise a virgin friend to have sex before marriage? Give a brief explanation of your answer.

9. Do you regret having sex before marriage?

10. Do your parents know?

11. If you could be a virgin again, would you? Does it matter?

Survey Answers — #2

1. What is your age? **21**

2. What is your gender? **Male**

3. Are you sexually active? **Yes**

4. If not, why?

5. How old were you at the time of your first sexual encounter? **15**

6. Were you comfortable? Why or Why not?

    No, because I felt like I was peer pressured to do it.

7. How many partners have you had? **8**

8. Would you advise a virgin friend to have sex before marriage? Give a brief explanation of your answer.

    I wouldn't pressure them.

9. Do you regret having sex before marriage? **No**

10. Do your parents know? **Yes**

11. If you could be a virgin again, would you? **Yes**

12. Does it matter to you? **It doesn't matter, but I wish I had stayed a virgin longer.**

Survey Answers — #3

1. What is your age? **20**

2. What is your gender? **Male**

3. Are you sexually active? **No**

4. If not, why? **I may have a child on the way.**

5. How old were you at the time of your first sexual encounter? **16**

6. Were you comfortable? Why or Why not? **Yes, because I was eager to do it.**

7. How many partners have you had? **8**

8. Would you advise a virgin friend to have sex before marriage? **No**

9. Give a brief explanation of your answer. **Because it's not right and also you don't want to make that mistake (unwanted pregnancy).**

10. Do you regret having sex before marriage? **No, well kind of 50/50.**

11. Do your parents know? **Yes**

12. If you could be a virgin again, would you? **Yes**

13. Does it matter to you? **Because I'm older now and I look at sex differently.**

Survey Answers — #4

1. What is your age?   **27**

2. What is your gender?   **Male**

3. Are you sexually active?   **Yes**

4. If not, why?

5. How old were you at the time of your first sexual encounter?   **2**

6. Were you comfortable? Why or Why not?   **Yes, because it's natural.**

7. How many partners have you had?   **13**

8. Would you advise a virgin friend to have sex before marriage?   **No**

9. Give a brief explanation of your answer.   **Because I would not want them to feel pressured. I feel like that's something for them to decide.**

10. Do you regret having sex before marriage?   **No**

11. Do your parents know?   **Yes, of course**

12. If you could be a virgin again, would you?   **Yes, of course**

13. Does it matter to you?   **Because I'm in a relationship, sex is important if I feel a connection with a female.**

BIBLIOGRAPHY

Allender, Dan. *Intimate Allies: Rediscovering God's Design for Marriage and Becoming Soul Mates for Life* (Wheaton, IL: Tyndale, 1995): 308.

Bonstra, Heather. "Public Health Advocates Say Campaigning to Disparage Condoms Threatens STD Prevention Efforts," *The Guttmacher Report*, vol. 6, March 2003.

Bum, Robert W. Blum. Mothers' Influence on Teen Sex: Connections That Promote Postponing Sexual Intercourse. Minneapolis, MN: Center for Adolescent Health and Development, 2002.

Brown, Jane D. "Mass Media Influences on Sexuality, "Journal of Sex Research, vol. 39, February 2002.

Clark, Jeffry K., Rebecca A. Brey, and Amy Banter. "Physicians as Educators in Adolescent Sexuality Education," Journal *of School Health, vol. 73,* December 2003, pp. 389-91.

Clark, Shelia. "Parents, Peers, and Pressures: Identifying the Influences on Responsible Sexual Decision-Making," 2002, www.naswdc.org.

Clod, Maria. "School's Official Assails 'Gay Lifestyle,' Fairfax Letter Urges Revisions to Teaching," The *Washington Post,* Feb. 3, 2005.

Fretheim, Terence. "Genesis," *The New Interpreter's Bible Commentary,* Vol. 1. Nashville, TN. Abingdon Press. 1994.

Harvery, Linda P. "Homosexual Agenda Escalates in Public Schools," www.Newswithviews.com, July 15, 2001. Copyright © 2001 by Newswithviews.com.

Heitt, Pete. Sermon: "A Temptation from Paradise" (3/27/05).

Meeker, Meg. *Epidemic: How Teen Sex is Killing Our Kids.* Washington, DC: Lifeline Press, 2002.

National Institute of Child Health and Human Development, "Strong Religious Views Decrease Teens' Likelihood of Having Sex," March 2003. www.nichd.nih.gov

Rector, Robert E., Kirk A. Johnson, and Lauren R. Noyes, "Sexually Active Teenagers Are More Likely to be Depressed and to Attempt Suicide." Heritage Foundation: June 3, 2003.

Serendipity Bible, 10th Anniversary Edition, For Personal and Small Group Study, (Grand Rapids, MI: Zondervan Publishing House, 1996).

Subrahmanyam, Kaveri, etal. "Constructing Sexuality and Identity in an Online Teen Chat Room," *Journal of Applied Developmental Psychology,* vol. 25, Nov/Dec 2004.

Smith, Shepherd. "The Truth Must Get to Teens about STDs," The Institute for Youth Development, March 1, 2004, www.youthdevelopment.org.

USA Today "Study: Abstinence Pledges Not Reducing Rates of STDs," March 9, 2004.

Tillman, William Jr. *Understanding Christian Ethics: An Interpretive Approach*, (TN: Broadman Press, 1988).

Wells, Ken and Bonnie Szumski. Teen Sexuality, Opposing Viewpoints, Greenhaven Press (Thompson Gale, The Thomson Corporation) Farmington Hills, MI 48331-3535.

Wolpert Stuart. "Teenagers Find Information About Sex on the Internet When They Look for it – And When They Don't, UCLA's Children's Digital Media Center Reports," *UCLA News, March 14, 2005, http://newsroom.ucla.edu.*

CPSIA information can be obtained
at www.ICGtesting.com
Printed in the USA
FFOW05n0424150715

9 781498 437004